A BRIEF FAMILY HISTORY OF DROWNING

BRYCE EMLEY

Sonder Press
New York
www.thesonderpress.com

While this is essentially a work of creative nonfiction, some names, details, events, and/or incidents have been changed, slightly altered, or are largely fictitious.

ISBN 978-0-9997501-4-8

First U.S. edition 2019
Printed in the USA
Distribution via Ingram

Acknowledgments

Thanks to the following magazines, where several of these pieces were published in various forms:

Memorious: "Prayer for Salt"
Foundry: "Renderings (My Father as Icarus)"
CutBank: "Mother, Mother, Ocean"
Nimrod International Journal: "Thesis/Antithesis"
Narrative: "Prayer in Rain, Autumn Night"
Mid-American Review: "Diving Deep (My Father as Octopus)"
Tahoma Literary Review: "Parabiosis (My Father as Anglerfish)"
wildness: "A List of Waters"

I'm indebted to the Edward F. Albee Foundation, The Glen Workshop, and North Carolina State University for the resources, community, and time they provided for me as I worked on portions of this manuscript, as well as Dorianne Laux, Eduardo Corral, Vievee Francis, John Balaban, Belle Boggs, Toni Jensen, and Angela Pelster for their care, insight, and attention. I'm also grateful for the support and friendship of Sam Piccone, Leila Chatti, Tyree Daye, Marty Saunders, Chris Wiewiora, and my NC State cohort.

Many thanks to everyone at Sonder Press and to Elena Stiehler for selecting this manuscript and for her editorial eye.

Brooke, Brynne, Beau, and Dad—this is for all of you.

Mom, thank you, again, for giving me words. I hope you're hearing them.

To Erin: everything, always.

for Mom and Dad

A BRIEF FAMILY HISTORY OF DROWNING

CONTENTS

PRAYER FOR SALT

I ETCH MY NAME into the shore, watching the wash unwrite and keep unwriting.

There are so many ways to drown.

Even the sea can't know what becomes of its dead. Where do all those bones go when water is done remembering?

I want to inherit the salt, speak the waves' prayers, feel the ocean's language crashing in my mouth, saying:

Dive into my chest, stay as long as you can hold your breath.

RENDERINGS (MY FATHER AS ICARUS)

I WAS FOUR WHEN blood flooded my father's skull.

Today, only half his body works. His boats are dry-rotting in his yard.

I drive him to the lake when I visit. All he does is stare, as if waiting.

Miles away, the Atlantic is crashing.

I think the lake is also waiting.

He describes the day of his stroke as the day he fell out.

The most obvious theme in Brueghel's *Landscape with the Fall of Icarus* is neglect. Icarus's flailing legs are an afterthought; if his name weren't in the title, you'd probably never notice him. The lowly ploughman is a tower in the foreground, so large you might think he's the subject.

The indifferent fisherman on the shore is a stand-in for the viewer: either apathetic or unaware, he goes about living, suggesting our lack of empathy for the suffering of others, too caught up in our own small lives to notice even the most spectacular plights of others.

My father is as far from the ocean as he can be in a state that is practically an island. The ocean has become a story, an echo in the ear.

In the stroke's wake, stories have become a default language for him, the past a metaphor he's trained his tongue to relate when his mouth can't form the words he's thinking in the moment. These stories are always about him—or rather the he he was before the stroke, as if he could speak that man back into being.

He once told me he'd always wanted two tattoos: a ship on one arm and a compass on the other, so he could always make it home.

His mouth is always dry.

Icarus would have no myth without his fall. Though his failure to arrive home was at least a successful departure from his prison, which was itself a freedom. In the poem "Failing and Flying," Jack Gilbert uses this aspect of the tale as a conceit for a broken relationship, closing, "I believe Icarus was not failing as he fell, / but just coming to the end of his triumph."

When I visit, my father tells me repeatedly that he's nearly healed, that when God is finished healing him, he'll get his driver's license back, get his boats fixed, go to the ocean. My sisters and I know this is the fiction that makes living bearable, the facts of his past composing his body's mythology.

From William Carlos Williams's take on *Landscape*, a poem by the same name as the painting:

> . . . the sun
> that melted
> the wings' wax
>
> unsignificantly
> off the coast
> there was
>
> a splash quite unnoticed
> this was
> Icarus drowning

Where Gilbert argues what's important about Icarus is that he tried ("anything/worth doing is worth doing badly"), Williams suggests we may be ignoring the lessons of his story altogether.

For over two decades, my father has felt he exists in a body on the verge of change, like ice floating on a surface still too cold to melt it.

When I take him to the lake, he stays in his truck. For him, water is both a reminder of limitation and a source of optimism. For Icarus, it was also an ending waiting for a story.

I remember almost nothing of my father before his stroke. My earliest memory of him is watching my sisters lead his semi-conscious body to the living room floor, where I try to coax him into playing with me—a blanket tied to my neck, draped behind me like a cape.

W.H. Auden suggests in the poem "Musée des Beaux Arts" that the participants in *Landscape* weren't too busy to notice Icarus; they just chose to ignore him:

> In Breughel's Icarus, for instance: how everything turns away
> Quite leisurely from the disaster; the ploughman may
> Have heard the splash, the forsaken cry,
> But for him it was not an important failure; the sun shone
> As it had to on the white legs disappearing into the green
> Water . . .

Indifferent, ignorant, or falling?

Water was an escape for my father, restless in a house where four children and a wife awaited him. He's always worn his wedding band alongside an anchor pendant on a gold chain that never leaves his neck.

Even in our myths we're flawed, inescapably human. And we can't stop revising these failures, as if we might somehow escape them through the stories we make of ourselves. Icarus didn't fall because he was a bad listener; he was a bad listener so we could watch him fall.

And if he was a martyr to failure, the art immortalizing him is both celebration and elegy. He flew like a god and was buried in waves. Still we recreate his sinking on canvas, cast ourselves in his tragedy, cradle his bones in our mouths.

SLOW BIOLOGY (MY MOTHER AS GREENLAND SHARK)

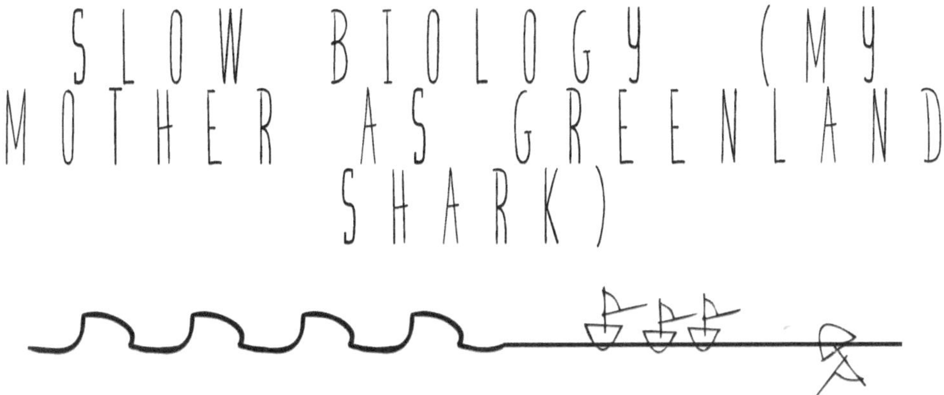

—after Angela Pelster

THINGS THAT TAKE THEIR time in living also tend to take their time in dying. Cold is one of nature's most effective agents for impeding life: winter is one example. The temperature of the North Atlantic Ocean can rest as low as 28 degrees Fahrenheit, water which, in most circumstances, is cold enough to no longer be called *water*. This is where the longest-living vertebrate on Earth lives and how it can live, for up to half a century.

Greenland sharks' skeletons are unusually soft; there are no calcified rings in their bones to age them the way marine biologists age other sharks: like trees. Instead, marine biologists have resorted to radiocarbon dating protein samples taken from tissue in the sharks' eyes, which is less accurate.

No researcher has been able to observe a specimen for long enough to record a full lifecycle, which is presumably longer than several generations of the researchers' own lifecycles combined.

Greenland sharks are adept predators. Once, one was found with an entire reindeer in her stomach. Another, most of a polar bear. But because of the nature of their environment—how cold it is, how deep—they are not considered a threat to humans.

Researchers are conducting an indefinitely long study on the effects of gradual aging in a small group of Greenland sharks. Through intense radiation treatments, the project's original researchers prompted the development of a small, malignant tumor in a 223-to-247-year-old female specimen called Mary. After decades of monitoring, the project's later researchers have reported practically no increase in the size of Mary's tumor.

Imagine: virtually immortal creatures with mouths the size of bears, a forest of teeth circling a glass tank. The water nearly arctic. Water so cold it seems always on the verge of becoming ice. When you test it with your hand, it feels somehow tenuous, as if the warmth from your body is all that is keeping it from freezing solid. Your fingers can barely move, even after just a few seconds of submersion. In this place, you could rest, and rest, and rest.

Because of their environment—its darkness—Greenland sharks' vision is poor. Their sense of hearing is acute, however, and they communicate using low-frequency sounds nearly inaudible to humans. Researchers often classify these sounds as *cries*. In one paper, these cries are compared to the sound ice makes as it melts on a wooden table.

If you ever see a Greenland shark, you will notice it appears to have an almost human-like mouth. It seems always to be open, speaking.

For ethical reasons, research on Mary's tumor was discontinued in the early 1990s. Mary was released back into the wild, at the time in almost perfect health.

Greenland sharks: of the family *Somniosidae*: sleeper sharks: who move so slowly their movement looks like sleep: who live so slowly their death is its own lifetime.

Researchers had hoped to apply to humans what they learned from Mary. "Creatures known almost ubiquitously for their capacity for destruction and consumption," one researcher argued in *Havforskning*, a prominent Norwegian marine science journal, in 1977, "could teach humans much about living."

It could be argued that to outlast an illness, to succumb to something else instead, is to survive it. If we could understand the language of Greenland sharks, maybe they would tell us to live slowly, not fearing the vast, cold darkness ahead; so slowly the world seems frozen around us, our own ages untraceable and unnoticed, our bodies suspended where they are and then gone.

It is possible death could be treated by slowing its approach, and perhaps this is the most we should hope for: even Greenland sharks must one day sink gradually into the hollow, colorless deep. It is possible Greenland sharks could teach us a more careful way to die. It is possible that to this day, somewhere in the North Atlantic Ocean, there is a Greenland shark with a name given to her by scientists, living with an easy, inhuman indifference to the silence growing in her gut, growing so slowly she does not notice it even with her acute sense of hearing, growing so slowly.

TROPIC

Everyone who is born holds dual citizenship,
in the kingdom of the well and in the kingdom of the sick.
—*Susan Sontag,* Illness as Metaphor

ONE NIGHT I STAYED to watch her: not sleep, but waiting.

A hospital is a barge between kingdoms.

It felt good to feel needed.

I think love is always selfish before we get it right.

I think our bodies learn to ache for passage.

Maybe we long for places, or we're the place itself: countries, like all islands, that break where they end.

A baby alligator crawled by her window at dawn.

Whatever happened felt like it could mean something.

It was Florida, and an orange tree was blooming.

It was lovely.

PARABIOSIS (MY FATHER AS ANGLERFISH)

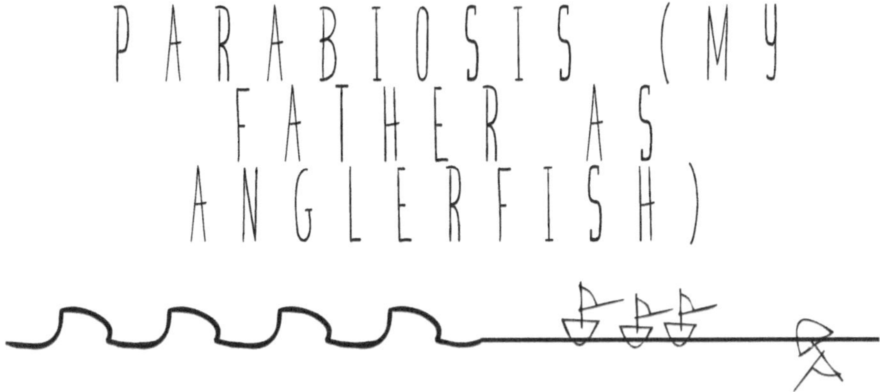

How do you know, wife, whether you will save your husband?
—I Corinthians 7:16

THE ADULT FEMALE ANGLERFISH is larger, more developed, more mature than the male.

He who finds a wife finds what is good

Latched to her is what appears to be a parasite. This is the male anglerfish, *Ceratiidae*, or "sea devil."

In this same way, husbands ought to love their wives
as their own bodies

The female is less than colorless: blanched, a paleness, a ghost dragging itself through deep water. There is immense pressure.

This is now bone of my bones and flesh of my flesh;

she shall be called

Mating requires a sacrificial unity: the male bites into her side, digests her flesh, fuses himself to her. This is shared blood, a becoming body.

Take, eat

The male grows, is kept because he provided,

...what God has joined together,
let man not separate

their offspring inheriting the darkness, hungering.

PRAYER IN RAIN, AUTUMN NIGHT

ONCE, SOMEONE TOLD ME I have a small heart.

When I weep I press the moment like a garlic clove. I want to feel, God I want to feel, how everything alive becomes a landscape.

Show me darkness, the color of the space between my ribs.

Show me darkness, the terrible mercies at the seasons' ends.

Let me long for more than the world I love too much to leave behind.

Let it be enough that everything looks alive when dressed in water, that so much living is most beautiful when it's dying.

MOTHER, MOTHER, OCEAN

You are the kind of guy who always hopes for a miracle at the last minute.
—*Jay McInerney,* Bright Lights, Big City

IT'S 11 A.M. YOU WERE driving until 4 a.m., but you're here now and awake.

Reusable containers holding variously palatable foods are crowding the counters. The counters are usually clean, vacant, as you recall. None of the containers are your mother's.

You recognize what these things often signify.

You eat cake.

Your mother's hospital room seems alive. There is beeping and pulse and mechanical hum. There are tubes.

When you speak into her ear she nods, pants "Okay" with the abruptness of the breathless. This seems the only word she can say.

You tell her things you've never said to her, things you want to be sure she knows. Everyone is saying it's important that you do this, though it seems like something people do in direr circumstances than you are convinced these are.

By afternoon, she no longer nods, or pants "Okay" when you speak to her.

Your father tells you and your sisters that your mother never told him her cancer had come back. Brynne reminds him that he went to chemo treatments with her, that this is the third time it has come back. He says he didn't know.

When you were four, blood flooded your father's brain, so you assume the two of them must be talking about different things. This happens sometimes, because of the flooding. It sounds like water when he speaks.

After your mother's first diagnosis in 2008, your sisters began researching holistics. Brooke tells you that grief and the lungs are connected. People with other internalized emotions—hatred and resentment, for example—tend to have issues with other organs—the pancreas, for example.

There has been much grief in your mother's life, but when Brooke talks about grief and your mother's lungs, she means your father.

Fluid on the lungs is a term you've heard them use—the doctors, your sisters. It isn't the cancer that concerns people, but this.

No one tells you what the fluid is. All you know is that there's a flood inside her chest, that when she takes a breath you can feel it bubble beneath her ribs, that every time she breathes it sounds like drowning.

When people visit, they want to know what happened. You recite a timeline you didn't participate in, pieced together from Brynne and your father: Monday she was fine; Tuesday she was sick; Wednesday she was too weak to text Brynne about being sick; Thursday the doctor sent her to the ICU; Friday she ate breakfast, her first meal in three days.

Saturday, you are here.

Aunt Esther calls your mother's phone. You hold it up to your mother's ear, check for silences on the other end. It sounds like a prayer.

You blink and there's a dampness. It feels foreign, sudden, the way rain does when the sun is out. There aren't many occasions one must do things like this.

Later, a teacher from you high school shows up. "She's a fighter," he says. "I mean if anyone can get through this..."

"I know."

"Just, the things she's been through. Beau and your dad and work, and this on top of it."

"…"

"… She was such an inspiration to Kerri, back when—when we were going through some things. She would tell me how just being around your mom, she got so much strength from her."

"Thank you."

"You know, I want you to know your dad wasn't—you were too young to know him before, but when I was starting out, I'd be up in front of the class, nervous as hell, and he'd check in and fire off jokes to the kids, ask if I needed anything. He was always joking. Always willing to help."

"…"

"I just wanted you to know—"

Her arms thrash wildly, as if she's swimming. If you don't hold them down she pulls at her oxygen mask and its tubes. She makes noises that sound like pleas. You hold her arms down. The oxygen continues. The swimming stops. When you release, she starts thrashing again and continues until you hold her down or until the nurse returns with Dilaudid.

You spend much of the day holding your mother.

"She is *guh*, she's *guh* person, *good people*."

Your father says variations of these phrases over and over until you only know what he's saying because you've just heard the words as words, and not as the wash of sounds they become in his mouth.

You spend the night in the room with your mother. You sleep in a faux-leather chair that doesn't so much recline as tilt. You sleep through the nurses turning your mother hourly. You sleep through the loud, young night-shift nurse with the large body and wild beard talking at your mother. You sleep through sunrise and shift change. You can't be sure all of these things happened, but it's likely.

It exhausts you to simply exist here, even for a night, even with your full and empty lungs.

The doctor tells you and your sisters and father that recovery would be a miracle. You understand that this is euphemistic. Your father listens, in his way.

The doctor also tells you this seems like torture, her breathing. *Breathing* is a more subjective term than you had considered. The oxygen mask is doing what her body is not. This is something of a loophole in the DNR/DNI.

These are difficult conversations. You all agree to continue them tomorrow.

Helena is the nurse you see most. She goes to church with your parents. She's slight, and serious. When she asks questions, you answer but she continues to look at you as if expecting more. This makes you uncomfortable.

When your mother starts thrashing again, Brooke goes looking for Helena and finds her crying in a utility closet.

It's after midnight, and you're home. You take a walk. When you lived here you did this often.

For no conceivable reason, you imagine that when you walk past your high school ex-girlfriend's house, her father might be outside, though you've never seen him out this late. He's a religious man. You think he might say, "Is that *you*?"

When you walk by he's on his doorstep making brittle noises. He gets up, dumps a dish's contents into the yard.

"Is that *you*?" He hugs you. He offers you shelled nuts. "They're almonds—a Biblical nut."

Inside, you begin to tell him everything. He stops you.

"A miracle, the doctor said?"

You nod.

"The doctor." He laughs. "Miracles happen, man. I'm tellin' ya." He tells you some. They are inexplicable.

A bird starts singing in the corner of the room. You hadn't noticed it before. Even your high school ex-girlfriend's father seems to notice it for the first time.

"You know that bird only sings when I'm in-tune with God, when I hit on something that's aligned with His Word."

You aren't sure how to respond.

"There are no coincidences. Do you believe that?"

You say you do.

"I mean I can't sleep, so here I am outside eating almonds, a *biblical nut*, and you happen to walk by. You can't make this stuff up."

You agree that you can't.

"You know Jeremiah?"

You say you do.

"Jeremiah one: The word of the Lord came unto me, saying, Jeremiah, what do you see? And I said, I see a rod of an almond tree. Then said the Lord unto me, You have seen well, for I will hasten my word to perform it."

He gives you his card, tells you he wants to anoint your mother tomorrow.

You walk home and your skin feels like rain.

Everybody has been telling you she is the strongest woman they know. And you think it, too, and that there are different ways to be strong. Her body needs some of these ways, others less so.

It's morning.

Swinging his inept right leg, your father moves slowly. You try to be slow, which becomes a practice in frequent standing. You want to tell Brooke about your high school ex-girlfriend's father and the almonds and the bird, but you have to wait for your father. He won't remember how to get to your mother's room on his own.

When you reach the ICU doors your phone rings. You are close enough that if Brooke were to speak louder, you could hear her twice: as she speaks into her phone from your mother's room and again, as those words come through your phone's speaker.

She tells you you should come in.

When you leave the hospital, everything looks remarkably the same as it did.

It's morning.

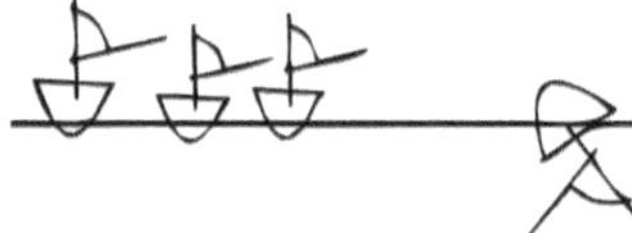

As you drive home from the hospital, your father tells you that other women in town "wanted" him. For the first time it sounds as if this statement isn't about him. Or, for the first time, it occurs to you to think that.

Your father also tells you that you and your sisters are all he has now. That you will go back to school and Brynne will go back to her baby and Brooke will simply go and he will have nothing left. Beau will be in prison for, at minimum, another fourteen years. Your father doesn't mention him.

It begins to feel like there is a dam inside your chest, bulging. When you are not talking to people you pretend to recognize, you need other things to do. You eat stale doughnuts, study your skin in a mirror, let out the dogs, watch college basketball, make sandwiches, take out the trash, read emails, etcetera. These feel like things you might otherwise be doing.

What a stroke is and what it means become different things. You are fairly certain you once heard that your father sustained frontal lobe damage. You know the frontal lobe is the small continent of the brain where reasoning dwells, where the things that make us human happen.

Your father says again that she never told him anything, but she told you things. You explain that no one knew she was dying. It wasn't the cancer, it was the pneumonia, the fluid. He says he didn't know that.

This happens several times daily and you feel the dam inside your chest, how it groans. Your father says his mind is foggy. "It *fah-yee*," he says. "I want to talk and it's *fah*, it's *fah*—I try to talk and it's just *fog*."

You realize your mother's house is saturated with clutter: half-finished to-do lists, newsletters, magazines, coupons, envelopes with phone numbers written on them. In the patio there's a stack of empty cardboard boxes; in a desk a Ziploc bag full of phone chargers. There are bags of new clothes in your nephew's size and many bags of old clothes. There are spare lids, spare washers, loose screws, potentially useful plastic pieces, reused tinfoil, empty film canisters.

All this has seeped slowly into your mother's home. Because she relegated these things to drawers, cabinets, spare rooms—places you rarely look—you never noticed its growth, its absurd excess, what that meant.

While staying with your mother at the Mayo Clinic in 2009, you learned that your father had told your mother—lighter by four lymph nodes and half a lung—that she should lose fifteen pounds.

He says nothing like this about her now. Instead, he has stories about girls, about frantically dressing as a father pulled into a driveway, about a trailer park neighbor asking him if he had a "big dick," about skirts pulled up, about "necking." He tells many of these to Pastor Simpson when he visits.

Brooke tells you about the talk she gave your father about what is respectful and appropriate.

You think these stories may be his language now, units of expression he uses to say what he otherwise has no words for because of the stroke and the frontal lobe. You tell this to Brooke. She's angry.

You think over your theory again and again. You must remind yourself that it could make sense, given the frontal lobe.

You hope that your father sustained frontal lobe damage.

"She nev—*she ne'er...*" Your father grunts. "I'm sorry. I'm just fah—it's fah-yee. I try to say something, and it's just fog."

The men in the immediate family of the deceased are expected to wear suits to funeral services—black shoes and black ties, not faded skinny chinos and tennis shoes and a dark brown tie.

The mall in West Palm Beach has all of those black things, including the same pair of shoes you already own but chose to leave three states away, along with your black tie and black pants and suit jacket—things you remember staring at in your closet while packing and deciding not to take because of what it would mean.

You keep thinking about the to-do lists, how many there were, how none were complete.

The morning of the funeral, your father calls you into his room to write words in a notepad for him: *superlatives, Louisiana, Notre Dame, dorm.* You recognize these as keywords in some of his stories, the ones in which he is popular in high school, in which Catholic girls undress him, in which girls hike their skirts up to get A's, in which he flunks out of Wake Forest, in which he crashes his first Austin Healey, in which Kathy Krause leaves him for a Notre Dame student who beats her, in which he scouts Oral Roberts freshmen for a date to a party.

Beau wasn't granted furlough, so Brynne recorded him speaking through the house phone into her cellphone. The church's sound lady plays it over the speakers during the service.

"After Dad's stroke, Mom continued to raise four kids and then even had to raise her husband. And she never stopped, never complained. That would be too ordinary, only humans do that."

There seems nothing else to say after your brother says these things.

Suddenly your father rises, holding a notepad. Brynne asks if anyone knew he would do this. Brooke shifts in her seat. There's talk of stopping him. His voice is a puddle on his tongue. He's telling stories you'd hoped he wouldn't, the stories he has told you for over two decades. For the first time they are told together, consecutively, or for the first time, you listen to them all as one story. Brooke keeps looking at you. Everyone is quiet. Everyone is listening. They laugh when he laughs. You are shifting. Brynne asks if you're going to stop him. Everyone is listening. You want him to stop, but you think this is important. Brooke is gesturing. You are listening and restless. There is the dam in your chest. Your father is talking, despite the puddle. Pastor Bruce puts an arm over his shoulder, thanks him. Your father sits and people are clapping.

It rained the day your mother died. Someone says the two events are related.

It has rained every day since, continues through the internment.

When you ask others about your father's funeral speech, they assure you it was hardly comprehensible but they got the gist, though they weren't sure about the part about the short skirt.

There are many people in the house, including Uncle Don, a gospel artist who pastors and church-goers regard as a kind of celebrity. He performs a three-song medley on the church piano during the service, culminating in his best-known song, "God Will Make a Way."

Now, Uncle Don is holding his phone between his head and your father's, playing Jimmy Buffet's "A Pirate Looks at Forty," your father's favorite song. Uncle Don is singing the words; your father is slurring them into melody, a moist, throaty sound, his eyes glossed into wet stones.

Mother, mother, ocean,
I have heard you call.

You recognize that this should be an affecting moment.

You're reading poetry as NFL draft predictions play on the TV. It's late, everyone is gone. Above the discussion of Jameis Winston's professional prospects, you hear your father speaking across the house but not to the only other person in the house, which is you.

He's not speaking the way people speak to others from across a house, projecting.

You look back to the poem you're reading. It closes: "Who would think / it was ever just us."

You turn the knob to make the shower hotter. The stream is a hailstorm of small fires on your skin. You turn the valve again, you are still unsure. You keep turning until the valve stops. You are surprised at the heat, how you can bear it.

How the burn becomes steam, and you breathe it.

The towels in the bathroom are new. There is a task at hand, to get dry. This is something you can do. There is no ceremony, no speaking, no waiting, no one.

There must be no softer towel in the world.

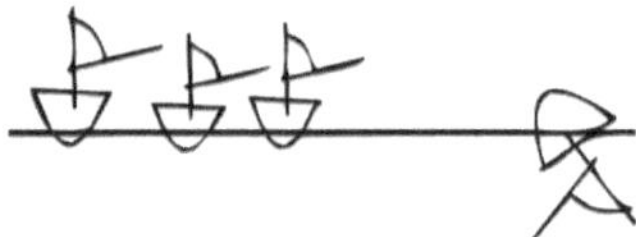

Grieving is referred to as a process.

Precipitation is another process, which is similar, in its way.

A few days later, someone asks you, "When she would wake up and move her arms, did you think it looked like she was swimming?"

"Yes."

"And when she inhaled, that it sounded like she was drowning?"

"Yes."

"There was fluid in her lungs, and she couldn't breathe. It probably felt like she was drowning."

"..."

"I wanted to say that, but I thought it would be hard for you."

"..."

"Maybe she was dreaming about drowning."

It's your father's birthday.

You and your sisters give him a card and a bag of Twizzlers. He seems appreciative.

From an Oliver Sacks essay you learn that the actor Spalding Gray sustained frontal lobe damage in a car crash and was prone to being "submerged in his memories and fantasies" after. Often, he would stare into deep bodies of water, purposeful. He would later throw himself from a bridge.

Brooks tells you your father was thinking of leaving your mother after you were born. Later he will tell you this was before you were born. But you don't know who he is because of the frontal lobe, and because you were four when it flooded.

Your father asks if you'd like to go with him on a drive. He takes you to the lake and parks. He tells you he comes out here often, that some days he sits for hours, "Just looking."

He gets out. You switch seats and drive home.

Your father tells you he knows it's not right, but he'd rather go ahead and be with your mother. He says Aunt Susan told him what heaven is like and it sounds like a neat place.

Instead, he goes up to Orlando with Brooke. This isn't ideal for anyone, particularly Brooke. But it will work, the way treading water does, for now.

Spalding said that his mind was filled with fantasies of his mother, and of water, always water.

"Why water, why drowning?" I asked.

"Returning to the sea, our mother," he said.

There's a leather-bound devotional on your desk. Aunt Susan gave you and your sisters each a copy. It's the same one your mother was reading with Beau, discussing over the phone every day. You open it to today's date: *I have promised to meet all your needs according to My glorious riches.* This seems a divine message, which helps.

April 3rd seems equally divine. As do April 4th and June 19th and August 7th and December 29th.

In Beau's recording at the funeral, he'd said that the morning after they told him about your mother, he opened his devotional. It was March 24th. It read, *This is a time in your life when you must learn to let go of loved ones.* He said he knew this wasn't a coincidence. He said there are no coincidences.

A week passes before you call your father. He says he knows what he wants to say, but it's still *fah-yee, still fah*—it's just *fog.*

When you were in the hospital, Brooke told you that when she was a child your mother used to pray Psalm 23 with her. You don't know if she still prays, but she told you she prayed the first verses over your mother, over and over.

The Lord is my shepherd; I shall not want. He makes me to lie down in green pastures: He leads me beside still waters. He restores my soul: He leads me in the paths of righteousness for His name's sake.

You have begun to admire the ocean, how it contains, is contained.

The monitor didn't flat-line that morning like you would have expected. It continued pulsing in waves, in-time with some other rhythm, indifferent.

You can recall this clearly.

Imagining her feels like holding water. It isn't pain. It is a lack in your own weight, as if you are sinking.

THESIS/ANTITHESIS

for my sisters; after Immanuel Kant

Thesis: just to be here is enough

FROM PRISON, MY BROTHER gives a eulogy through church speakers. Another absence at the end of a voice that told me once he had the devil in his head, says that now he walks with God, talks of angels. I say nothing—jealous of his grief, how much more of it he has, the altar so crowded with calla lilies her casket seems buried in light.

Antithesis: we are never here enough

As her respirator lullabied, I came home one night so high I fell asleep on the driveway. I woke for dinner and she showed me her legs, how the rashes flowered blood-sick. She asked me for blessing. We bowed our heads, searched plates for proof of hunger, the difference between waiting and prayer.

Thesis: our dreams are where we're haunted

Sick of dreaming, we don't sleep. One sister lies awake reading books in foreign languages, the other picks her fingers raw. I stay up watching spiders appear between the cracks in the siding of my house, admire how they trust the darkness just enough to test it, how they move with such grace that they're closer before I notice.

Antithesis: dreaming brings the dead to us

When I sleep I see her body in shallow water, hear a voice draining from a mouth full of salt. I wake, my head brimming fog, and wait for haunting, dream of sage and brittle stars, or only sleep.

Thesis: grief is a shared weight

We don't talk much, except of how it finds us at our desks at night, in the produce aisle, the shower. How sometimes breath gets to feel so heavy in our chests. How we can't quite name what is pulling us so gracefully into the earth.

Antithesis: grief is our own transcription

This is a loner's cryptography, a fevered alphabet so someone else might feel the heat of my skin while I describe the burning. I want to craft a language of her ghost, catalogue her absence, the matter of her, how her letters smelled like echinacea and lavender and her hand was so lovely I could barely read it.

Thesis: a mother is the home we're always returning to

I can't stop feeling heartsick for a time that hasn't come yet. Don't think I know what grief is, if not the guilt and awe of knowing what the dead unlearned before us. I don't miss them anymore. It isn't that. I miss the missing, that little exorcism, how once she was gone all I wanted was to sleep inside every abandoned house I saw.

Antithesis: a mother is the home we leave behind

I want to know the awful kindness of unmaking yourself, being the place another used to be. How can we ever make it back? I saw her body as a rusted river and when I called to her, she sang through a mouth full of clay—I can't even dream right anymore. So far from the one who named me, from the room I hollowed into her, a trickle that carves a canyon from the earth.

TO INMATE K62912, JACKSON C.I.

—for Beau

FROM AN EMPTY BAR in a desert city, I'm writing a letter I won't send, watching rain, the weather of our growing up.

Always a storm cloud in your blood, a wild crashing—I still tend to love the things I fear.

We made ditches our domain. Plywood ship and palm frond oars, I remember almost nothing else for years.

The quiet heart of all that youth has cracked in the drought of you. Mom was holding in her breath.

You were named *beautiful,* in a language we don't speak.

I think it must have been a prayer.

FROM INMATE K62912, JACKSON C.I.

I'VE FOUND PRAYER HERE is no release.

For once, all I do is stay. Even the weather is privileged.

But I want the sky before the storm, domain of all that fearless youth.

I remember almost nothing but endings, the calm once the breath is caught again. I've been sick with crashing, the ripple in a puddle growing more into itself. You could drown that way.

Brother, there's water in my name, can you hear it?

A gentleness, the pool of our mother's mouth.

DIVING DEEP (MY FATHER AS OCTOPUS)

from Peter Godfrey-Smith's essay "On Being an Octopus: Diving Deep in Search of the Human Mind"

How do we approach questions about what it's like to be something or someone?

THE BLEEDING IN HIS brain taught him the distance between what is thought and what can be said—channels flooded, words wet-blurred as they surface on his tongue. I only ask what it's like to be him in a diving bell.

Getting a sense of what it feels like to be another animal—bat, octopus, or next-door neighbor—must involve the use of memory and imagination to produce what we think might be faint analogues of that other animal's experiences.

I once found his scuba gear in the attic—tank specked with rust, tubes stiff with rot, gauge shot to hell—and brought the mouthpiece to my lips.

...early researchers inferred that the arms [of octopuses] have a good degree of independence from the central brain.

Paralysis is a sort of independence: flesh refusing to feel, a knee bending only for gravity, a hand clasped always into seashell, too stubborn to carry any of the fishing poles now brittle in his shed. It's not phantom limb, what's lost continually proving its absence. It's lips chasing shadows gliding on their surface, the tongue crashing like a breaker back into itself.

To work out what it might feel like to be another animal, we have to find some way to justify mappings between what goes on inside that animal and experiences we can ... [only] partly conjure in ourselves.

Father who speaks as a child, who reasons as a child, whom I know as a child—how my brother would wrap me in a sheet and pin me to the floor, how my blood thrashed inside me and my voice flooded my teeth. It felt like drowning. These men must always feel like drowning. How we have all ached for release.

If octopuses did not exist, it would be necessary to invent them.

Rorschach's spills taught us we create what we know, invention filling the need that invented it. Seed to son, thought to word, father to *my* father—every word an inkblot blossoming, a small invention itself inventing.

What is it like to be an octopus?

This is as close as it gets: pulling down the attic's stairs, a light bulb's *click*,

A LIST OF WATERS

—*after Tyree Daye*

i.

THE TRUTH IS I'M sick of my blood. How I must be in some way the man who would teach a husband's power is the sound of crashing in his throat, that we're water's second try at the world.

ii.

We get our turn at being young, becoming the people we love because we have to.

Hold our fathers like storms inside us.

Break our mothers open just to be here, asking.

iii.

When I talk about men, I always mean my father, who couldn't help wearing his skin like an ethos, whose love takes the shape of its container, who can't remember holding his wife by the throat like a bouquet of waterlilies.

iv.

I learned from my mother a wife is an anchor's chain, a marriage is what holds you under.

v.

When I talk about fathers, I always mean river. Or the other way around, we know them the way we read the earth where water has been.

vi.

Father who only knew to love poorly, I've loved worse: a likeness with no weight to ripple the surface.

As if even neglect were a form of intimacy: like faith, not felt, just a longing to feel.

vii.

The truth is, any truth is just a version.

The truth is, a son is a dry basin.

Is it wrong to love a man for what he's made?

If not love, know.

If not love, rend.

If not love, river.

If not love.

PRAYER FOR CROSSING

IF WE WAKE, WE to your silence, a glass bell pleading for a tongue.

But I'm praying neglect is just a voice the wrong shape for our ears, that we've been shouting from the far country for more than just to know we're here.

We wash our hands in the river, share our mouths with the wind. All our light is borrowed. We're as sturdy and as loud as shadows here, where the present is a harbor we're always arriving at.

This is what I tell myself of grief: like all borders, imagined.

Let there be a coda to this coda, let there be ships.

Let these small seas in our chests crash against a shoreline where they end.

Author Note

Bryce Emley was born and raised in Florida and earned an MFA in Poetry from North Carolina State University. His poems, essays, and fiction appear in *The Atlantic, Boston Review, Prairie Schooner, Narrative, Best American Experimental Writing,* and elsewhere, and he is also the author of the poetry chapbook *We Might Never Be This Beautiful Again* (Seven Kitchens Press, forthcoming) and the fiction chapbook *Smoke and Glass* (Folded Word, 2018). A recipient of residencies and scholarships from the Edward F. Albee Foundation, The Glen Workshop, Wesleyan Summer Writers Conference, and the University of Central Florida, Bryce is Poetry Editor of Raleigh Review and works in marketing at the University of New Mexico Press. He lives in Albuquerque, NM with his wife. Read more at bryceemley.com.

www.ingramcontent.com/pod-product-compliance
Lightning Source LLC
Chambersburg PA
CBHW032011120726
47902CB00014B/2080
9780999750148